More Animals

More Animals

BY OLIVER HERFORD

with Pictures by
the Author

Dover Publications, Inc., New York

Published in Canada by General Publishing Company, Ltd., 30 Lesmill Road, Don Mills, Toronto, Ontario.

Published in the United Kingdom by Constable and Company, Ltd., 10 Orange Street, London W.C. 2.

This Dover edition, first published in 1966, is an unabridged and unaltered republication of the work originally published by Charles Scribner's Sons in 1901.

Standard Book Number: 486-21648-9

Library of Congress Catalog Card Number: 66-23392

Manufactured in the United States of America
Dover Publications, Inc.
180 Varick Street
New York, N.Y. 10014

Contents

Contents—*Continued*

More Animals

The Tortoise.

The Tortoise.

THE Tortoise is, to say the Least,
A very Contradictory Beast.
Though he may walk the wide world o'er
He cannot step outside his Door.
The Slowest Creature 'neath the Sun
He's Noted for a Race he Won.
Ignoblest of Created Things
His Shield has Many Quarterings,
And Lastly, though Devoid of Hair
His Combs are Famous everywhere.

Tortoise

The Crocodile.

The Crocodile.

OH, shun the Crocodile, my Child ;
He is not Tractable and Mild,
Nor like the Dog, the Friend of Man.
He's built upon a Different Plan,
He is not Diffident or Shy,
He will not shrink when you say "Fie !"
And though he's said Sometimes to Cry,
Be not Responsive to his Wail,
Nor Pat him if he wag his Tail.
This Picture's true to Every Line
Except the Smile. (The Smile is mine.)

The Crocodile

The Tiger.

The Tiger.

Now Comes the Tiger, Fierce and Bold,
His Doublet slashed with Black and Gold.
He loves to Roar and Rant and Rage
Upon the Jungle's Tragic stage,
Where he holds Undisputed Sway
As Leading Villain of the Play,
His Style is Real, and Intense;
Yet though he Moves his Audience
He is not Popular at all
(He never had a Curtain Call).
Whoever stays to see the End
Will never more the Play attend;
And when his acting goes Amiss,
Only the Cobra dares to Hiss.

A Tiger.

The Swan.

The Swan.

OH, see the Swan swim to and fro.
They say the Swan is Dumb. Oh, no!
It is Contraryness, a Crime
Common to Singers of Our Time.
She has a wondrous Vocal Gift,
And yet she does not deign to lift
Her Voice, lest Men should Criticise.
She will not Sing, until she Dies,
Nor will she then her Grave forsake
As Opera Singers do, to take
An Encore—and she makes but one
"Farewell Appearance."—When 'tis done
She sings no more. Is not the Swan
A Musical Phenomenon?

The Mouse.

The Mouse.

CONSIDER now the Humble Mouse.
He is an Outlaw in the House.
He makes his Hiding in the Wall
And lives upon the Crumbs that fall.
And yet, my Child, although we deem
The Mouse a Pest, he stands Supreme,
The Wonder of Creation's Plan,
The only Subject known to Man
Concerning which we're safe to find
No Woman ever Changed her Mind.

A Mouse

The Hen.

The Hen.

ALAS! my Child, where is the Pen
That can do Justice to the Hen?
Like Royalty, She goes her way
Laying Foundations every day
Though not for Public Buildings, yet
For Custard, Cake and Omelette.
Or if too Old for such a use
They have their Fling at some Abuse,
As when to Censure Plays Unfit,
Upon the Stage they make a Hit,
Or at Elections Seal the Fate
Of an Obnoxious Candidate.
No wonder, Child, we prize the Hen
Whose Egg is Mightier than the Pen.

HEN

The Tapir.

The Tapir.

THE Tapir is a *Pachyderm*,
To use a Scientific Term.
But if you meet him, don't allude
To such a word; not that it's Rude,
But, living in a Foreign Land,
The Tapir would not understand,
Having no Latin, and Less Greek,
And might an awful vengeance wreak,
Not dreaming "*Pachyderm*" implied
His own Invulnerable Hide.
Oh, *when* will Scientists see fit
To moderate their Terms a bit!

The Tapir

The Lion.

The Lion.

THE Lion is, if anything,
Even "more Royal than the King."
His Folks were Something in that Line,
Ere man invented *Right Divine.*
You wonder then how He can stoop
To things like Jumping through a Hoop.
Observe, my Child, He's not alone,
There is a Power Behind the Throne
Who Curbs His will, and Moulds His Views,
And makes Him mind His Ps and Qs.
Then if He's Good, she lets Him Take
From Her sweet Lips a Piece of Cake.
Ah, Child, it's very plain to see,
Kings are not what they used to be!

Lion

The Adjutant.

The Adjutant.

THE Adjutant, I may explain,
Is a Gigantic sort of Crane.
A Realist would dance with Rage
To see him pictured on this Page
Holding a gun, but though 'tis not
Exactly true, it adds a lot;
And that is where the Art comes in.
The Artist does not care a Pin
Always to follow Nature's Groove.
It is Art's Mission to Improve
On Nature, just as I have done.
But if you do not like the Gun,
And Realistic Art prefer,
Go then to a Photographer.

The Adjutant.

The Gnu.

The Gnu.

BEWARE, My Dear, if ever you
Should chance to come across a Gnu!
You may be Fair, and Tall, and Svelte,
But do not hope the Gnu to melt.
You may be Gentle, Kind, and True,
These Things mean nothing to the Gnu.
You may love Beasts, both Great and Small,
That won't affect the Gnu at all.
You may be Generous, you may
Subscribe to the S. P. C. A.,
All this of no avail will be,
The Only Thing's to Climb a Tree.
And if there *is* no Tree to Climb,
Don't say you were not warned in Time!

A Gnu.

The Zebra.

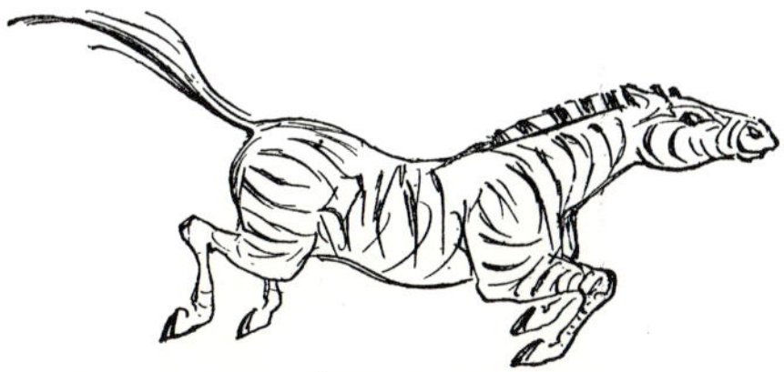

The Zebra.

A STORY Teller of Some Note
Before My Time, who also wrote
Of Animals, tells of An Ass
Who for a Lion tried to Pass.
But though he wore a Lion's Skin,
No one, of course, was Taken In.
Even as Æsop's Ass, so fares
The Zebra, for although he wears
The Tiger's stripes, he does not gain
The Tiger's strength, nor yet retain
The Simple Virtues of the Ass.
He Fails to Shine in either Class.
A Plagiarist, who but Befools
Himself, and falls between two Schools.

The Zebra.

The Horse.

The Horse.

THIS noble Beast—

    But, why discourse

Upon the Virtues of the Horse?
They are too numerous to tell
Save when you have a Horse to Sell.
No Beast has done so much as He
To elevate Society.
How *could* Society Get On
(Or off), my Child, if He were gone?
We Owe him Much, yet who can say
He ever asked us to Repay?
Ah, Child! How Bright the World would be,
If Creditors were All as He.

A Horse.

The Octopus.

The Octopus.

THE Devil fish, or Octopus,
Has often been Held Up to us
To typify the Greedy Lusts
Of Grasping Syndicates and Trusts.
This Picture (from an Early Print)
Gives us, if true, a Fearful Hint
Of his Great Size, and throws some Light
On his tremendous Appetite.
But let us, Child, whate'er we do,
Give the poor Devil fish his Due!
The Picture, I forgot to say,
Is Quite Untrue in every way.
The Moral's Plain as Plain can be:
Don't believe Everything you See.

Octopus.

The Camel.

The Camel.

THE Camel may be likened to
A Desert Ship. (This is not new.)
He is a Dangerous-looking Craft,
With Frowning Turrets, Fore and Aft.
A Cargo of no little bulk
He carries, too, on his great Hulk.
We little realize on Earth
How much we owe to his great Girth.
For should he ever Shrink so Small
As through the Needle's Eye to Crawl,
Rich men might Climb the Golden Stairs
And so leave Nothing to their Heirs.

A Camel

The Ant Eater.

The Ant Eater.

SOME to the Virtuous Ant may go
To Learn Her ways. Alas! not so
The Ant Eater, he Goes, indeed,
But only on the Ant to Feed.
Behold him, like Proverbial Swine,
On Living Pearls of Wisdom dine!
O, Virtuous Ant, whose Moral State
In Childhood's Hour we learned to Hate,
Whom Copybooks and Proverbs laud;
Unless you are a Pious Fraud,
In that Dark Moment when you glide
Into the Ant Eater's Inside,
The Thought some comfort may afford,
That Virtue is its *Own* Reward.

Ant-eater

The Shark.

The Shark.

THIS is the Shark, my Child, I pray
Do not Recoil or Turn Away;
'Tis true the Shark is not the Pink
Of nice Propriety, but Think!
Think of the Horrid Sailor Men
He *has* to Swallow now and then,
With all their Untold Yarns inside
And all their Fearful Oaths beside!
Put yourself in his place, my Child,
Could *you* keep Spotless, Undefiled?
If only we could make the List
Of those on whom He *should* subsist,
No Home, I'll venture to Remark,
Would be complete without a Shark.

A Shark.

The Frog.

The Frog.

BEHOLD the Frog, and then Contrast
His Present with his Humble Past!
Once but a Tadpole in a Pool,
Now nature's gayly Painted Fool.
So *Newly Rich* in Legs and Toes,
He's sadly lacking in Repose,
Yet He is never Impolite.
He hops and jumps from sheer delight,
And shows with each Gymnastic Spasm
The Convert's Fresh Enthusiasm.

Frog

The Bear.

The Bear.

THE Bear is not a Seemly Brute,
He lives on Berries, Nuts, and Fruit,
Although on Children he will Feed
When he is very Cross indeed.
An Ancient Tale may be Recalled,
How once a Prophet, Old and Bald,
Was by Irreverent Children mocked,
Whereat Two She Bears were so Shocked,
They fell upon those Children Rude,
And ate up all the Naughty Brood.

MORAL.

The Moral is avoid alway
A Prophet on his Busy Day.

The Bear

The Porcupine.

The Porcupine.

I LIKE the Fretful Porcupine—
Deception is not in his line.
With him there is no Makebelieve,
He wears his Thorns upon his sleeve.
Unlike some Human Porcupines
Who carefully Conceal their Spines,
His Bad Points stick out everywhere.
'Tis true he's Fretful as a Bear,
And Vainer than a Popinjay,
Yet has he One Redeeming Trait
That to my heart endears him quite:
Though full of Quills, *he does not write.*

Porcupine

The Cow.

The Cow.

THE Cow is too well known, I fear,
To need an introduction here.
If She should vanish from Earth's face
It would be Hard to fill Her place;
For with the Cow would disappear
So much that every one holds Dear.
Oh, think of all the Boots and Shoes,
Milk Punches, Gladstone Bags, and Stews
And Things too Numerous to Count
Of which my Child She is the Fount!
Let's hope, at least, the Fount may last
Until *Our* Generation's past!

A Cow

The Do-Do.

The Do-Do.

THIS Pleasing Bird, I grieve to own
Is now Extinct. His Soul has Flown
To Parts Unknown, beyond the Styx
To Join the Archœopteryx.
What Strange, Inexplicable Whim
Of Fate, was it to banish him?
When Every Day the numbers swell
Of Creatures we could spare so well:
Insects that Bite, and snakes that sting,
And many another Noxious Thing.
All these, my Child, had I my Say,
Should be Extinct this very Day.
Then would I send a Special Train
To bring the Do-do back again.

The Dachshund.

The Dachshund.

Part I.

The Dachshund is the Longest Dog
In the whole Canine Catalog.
He is so Long—to show him Here
He must in *Serial Parts* appear.
This is *Part One*—Observe his Air
Of Lack-a-daisi-cal Despair.
I fear he finds it does not Pay
To wag a Tail so Far Away,
He is so very Long and Low.
And yet he was not always so.
The Dachshund once was Tall and Fleet
As any Dog you'd wish to meet.
Alas! He met a Fearful Fate.
One Day—but we anticipate.

Continued.

Dachshund 1.

The Dachshund.

The Dachshund.

Part II.

And now, Dear Reader, we must go
Back some Six Thousand Years or So
To Eden's Lovely Garden, where
With an Historic Happy Pair
Lived the First Dachshund, Tall and Proud.
The Sign that reads "*No Dogs Allowed*"
Hung not in Eden's Garden Bright.
And all was Joyous, till One Night
The Faithful Dog awoke in Dread,
To find the Happy Pair had fled.
Madly he searched the Garden round
But not a Trace of them he found,
When Suddenly he saw a Sight
That made him Howl with Grief and Fright.

Continued.

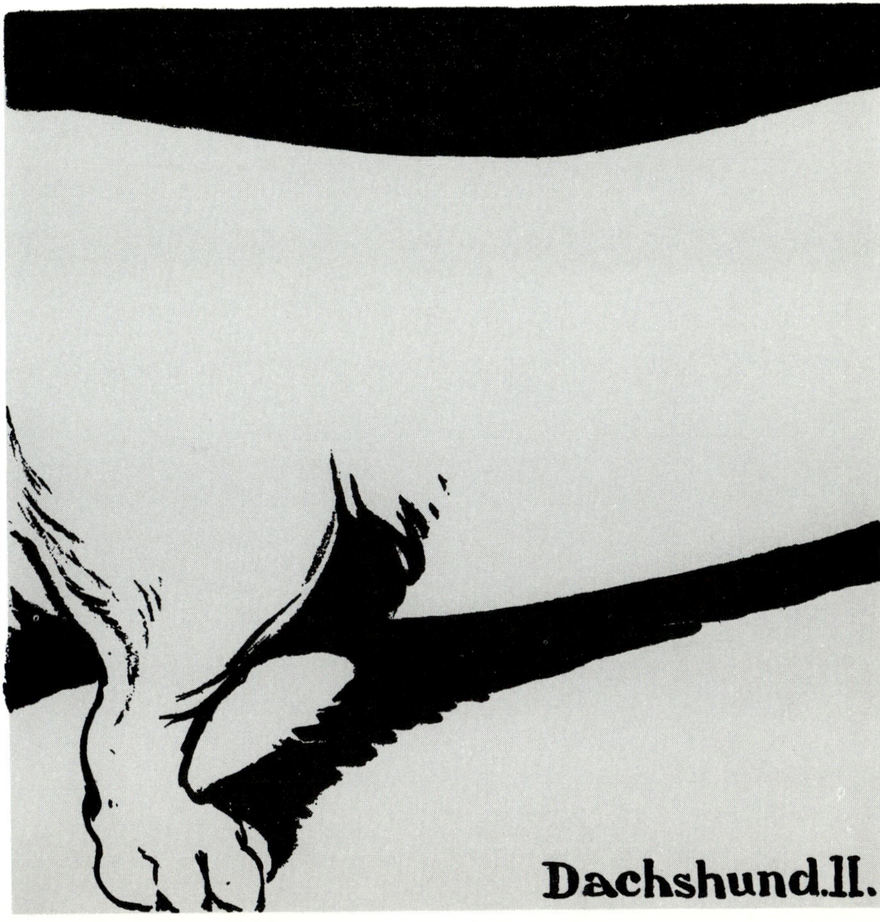
Dachshund.II.

The Dachshund.

The Dachshund.

PART III.

HE saw, with mingled Grief and Fear,
His Master and his Mistress Dear,
Thrust through the quickly closing Gate.
He sprang to join them, but too late!
In vain he tried to leap the Wall;
Only one Hope was left, to Crawl
Beneath the Gate. It happened here,
By just an inch or two, to clear
The ground. With Supercanine strength
He Squirmed and Squeezed, until at length,
When half way through,—unhappy luck!—
He could not move—in short, was stuck.
Here we must leave him to pursue
The fortunes of the Other Two.

Continued.

Dachshund III.

The Dachshund.

The Dachshund.

Part IV.

Unhappy Pair! Left to their Fate
In a Strange World, Outside the Gate
Without a single Friend; but hark!
What is that dear familiar Bark?
They pause a moment in their Flight
And see their Faithful Doggie's plight.
With willing Hands, and Patience too,
At last they pull him safely through.
But Oh, the Difference! No more
The Tall and shapely Hound of Yore—
This Strange, Flat Dog with Crumpled Feet.
But let us draw a veil discreet
Upon that meeting . . . Now we know
Why the Dachshund is Long and Low.

(THE END.)

Dachshund IV.